CW00749933

HowExpert Presents

Extreme Ironing 101

A Quick Guide on How to Extreme Iron Step by Step from A to Z

HowExpert with Marie Claire Medina

For more tips related to this topic, visit HowExpert.com/extremeironing.

Recommended Resources

- HowExpert.com – Quick 'How To' Guides on All Topics from A to Z by Everyday Experts.
- HowExpert.com/free – Free HowExpert Email Newsletter.
- HowExpert.com/books – HowExpert Books
- HowExpert.com/courses – HowExpert Courses
- HowExpert.com/membership – HowExpert Membership Site
- HowExpert.com/writers – Write About Your #1 Passion/Knowledge/Expertise & Become a HowExpert Author.
- HowExpert.com/resources – Additional HowExpert Recommended Resources
- YouTube.com/HowExpert – Subscribe to HowExpert YouTube.
- Instagram.com/HowExpert – Follow HowExpert on Instagram.
- Facebook.com/HowExpert – Follow HowExpert on Facebook.

Table of Contents

Introduction

The world of extreme sports is evolving every day. Many of us are reinventing the parameters of tradition and creating new ways to do things. In 2016, skateboarding was among several new sports added to the 2020 Olympic line up. Quite impressive if you think about the startup days of skateboarding. In the late 40's surfers wanted a way to "ride the waves" when there weren't any. Now, it is the new Olympic sport. Extreme ironists all around the world have the same aspiration for their sport.

This book is a step-by-step guide to extreme ironing. It covers all the bloopers and questions I encountered when first taking on this extreme sport. If you want to become an extreme ironist, break out of your comfort zone, master another extreme sport, conquer your fears, or you are just curious, read on!

Chapter 1: Extreme Ironing 101

What Is Extreme Ironing?

Extreme Ironing is any ironing done outside the traditional setting of indoors. But, most committed extreme ironists do not stop there. Eventually, you will want to graduate beyond the novice level of extreme ironing by mixing ironing with an extreme sport.

According to Phil Shaw, the man credited by many for coining this extreme sport, the definition of extreme ironing is, "sport involving ironing clothes outdoors in dangerous or unusual locations". Phil Shaw aka Steam, is said to have founded extreme ironing from his hometown of Leicester, England in 1997. Although, this claim might lead to some dissension with our ancient ancestors since they may have been extreme ironing with pans and hot coals long before the Heian period in Japan and China in the middle ages.

Until they come back to lay claim to the founding rights, the story goes something like this – One day, Phil is said to have taken his ironing chores to his backyard and extreme ironing was born.

Extreme Ironing History

Since its modern-day re-conception, the sport of extreme ironing has evolved and many have added on their own interpretation and purpose.

In 2007, Claudia Kappenberg of Brighton University, took to the streets of Darmstadt Germany to perform *Intervention*, an extreme ironing interactive performing art exhibit. The exhibition was a collaboration of 46 artists from around the world including Canada, Israel, and the United States. It engaged with viewers and appealed to philosophical elements of daily life. According to Claudia, "the work performs ritualistic activities or repetitive loops to challenge one system by creating another" .... "caught in these parameters we see, and experience, the body in terms of its utility, limiting our engagement with the world".

A more recent development in extreme ironing, was in 2016 by De Montfort University Leicester (DMU). One participating ironist said they were, "helping society break the myth: university students don't know how to iron".

Ironists all over the world continue to invent new purpose for this extreme sport. Some are searching for exhilarating connections with the forces of nature. Some are wanting to send a message that they know how to iron. Other extreme ironists are examining and altering the framework of convention. Then, there are those that have made it their mission to get more people involved and make this the next Olympic sport.

What is your motivation? Whatever it is, I will take you through some of my own experiences, what I have learned, and the basic 'how to' of extreme ironing.

What makes extreme ironing so unique is that it has become a limitless extreme sport. The rules of engagement are not defined, and this is exactly how ironists want it. Ironists continue to push the limit with this sport by learning from each other and consistently challenging each other to conquer life outside of the existing parameters. The list has no end! Extreme ironing on your surfboard while catching some waves, on a motorcycle, cycling, kayaking, stand-up paddle boarding, skiing, scuba diving, summiting the highest peaks. The list goes on.

While you are reading this extreme ironing guide, think of what sports you will want to do extreme ironing with or what setting you will want to be in. You can change it later, but having a setting or sport in mind will help you apply this 'how to' guide and get you on the right track to becoming an extreme ironist!

Chapter 2: Extreme Ironing Locations

Extreme ironing is any ironing done outside the traditional setting of indoors, but the ultimate extreme ironist knows the real definition of extreme lies in combining ironing with another outdoor sport. Whether it be hiking, cycling, rock climbing, parasailing, surfing, or scuba diving. You decide! Since the type of equipment will depend on your location, we are going to start by going over some locations. But, don't limit yourself; as I mentioned in the previous chapter, extreme ironing is limitless and you can do it all!

A great starting point is incorporating ironing with things you already do and enjoy. I started by taking ironing to the park and hiking; then, I moved on to scuba diving and mountain climbing. To become skilled at extreme ironing, it is going to take practice. Start where you are most comfortable, then, get creative and challenge yourself!

Parks & Campsites

Parks and campsites are great starting points for anyone curious about the sport. Before

I attempted extreme ironing for the first time, I watched a TEDx Talks video by an extreme ironist named Maki Sugimoto. In the video, Maki shares how fear once dominated his life and describes the feelings that raced through him the first time he extreme ironed.

It is not until you go out to a public place and start ironing that you will understand the connection many fellow extreme ironists have with this sport. By the time I finished walking past all the people in the park with my ironing board, setting my board upright, making that first press onto my shirt, I stopped counting all the pairs of eyes staring at me.

It didn't matter. It is like a special defibrillator for all your fears. You are shocked out of your embarrassment. There is no place to hide, you have to face it. You have to own it. That is when you start having fun!

In the picture on the previous page, I climbed on top of the Sweetwater Creek Ruins at Sweetwater Creek State Park, Georgia. These ruins were used as part of The Hunger Games: Mockingjay film set. When I have the time, I like to find parks with a lot of history or parks that have a unique set of challenges. Once you become comfortable enough with extreme ironing, start to look for parks with boulders, ruins, cliffs, and climbing trees (e.g. weeping willows, angel oak trees, crabapple trees, oak trees).

While at Sweetwater Creek State Park, I chose to plug in. I used a 100-foot extension cord and a portable generator. I will go over what 'plug in' means in another section of this chapter, but for now, you can reference this for later.

Another fun alternative option to parks are campsites. They are fully equipped with onsite facilities like toilets, showers, and electrical plug in capabilities. I consider them to be a step up from local parks. Due to the location and the variety of provisions, they are great for beginners. Campsites can lead to more extreme adventures than your local parks.

USCAmpgrounds.info is a great online resource for campgrounds across the United States and Canada. The website will even let you know what type of amenities each campground offers and what you'll need and won't need during your visit.

Parks and campgrounds will help you build the skills you will need to become a professional extreme ironist. If you are on the fence about this extreme sport or don't know what location to start at, head to your local park or a campground!

Urban, Suburban, Exurban Locations

Urban locations are densely populated locations, while suburban and exurban are locations outside the city, with exurban farther out than suburban. These are fun locations. They are local or road trip worthy adventures and because you are most likely to be seen, there is a lot of laugher involved and an interesting story to share at the end of the day.

For these locations, I use the saying, 'You know, this isn't crazy until you pull out the ironing board!' This sums up how most extreme ironists feel the moment they take out their board in public. This saying has become my hallmark and a hallmark for many other ironists. It can be compared to, 'on your mark, get set, go', because once an ironist is finished saying, 'You know, this isn't crazy until right now!' you have got to start. Your board is out, there is no hesitating.

At this location, I did not plug in because it was raining, but I was developing extreme ironing skills in various weather conditions. It was a successful extreme ironing day!

A lot of times these locations offer the same thrill as trekking a summit or skydiving. You do not have to travel far to earn extreme ironist credibility.

Below are a few locations, in the United States, to put on your extreme ironing bucket list:

Bodie Ghost Town, California

Murphy Ranch, California

Death Valley Salt Flats, California

Apple Boulders, California.

Denver Union Station, Colorado

The Labyrinth, Minneapolis

Utility Tunnels, Minnesota

Central Station, Michigan

Eastern State Penitentiary, Pennsylvania

Old City Hall Station, New York

Freedom Tunnel, New York

Central Railroad Terminal, New Jersey

I did not cover every state in the list above. You can use this list as a reference when researching places local to you.

Extreme & Global Locations

I believe Mount Everest, Mount Fuji, Angel Falls, Mount Kilimanjaro, and Moana Loa are the ultimate glory – crème de la crème – for an extreme ironist.

But, two of my favorite extreme ironing experiences were Doi Inthanon and Koh Bida Nok in Thailand. The highest peak in the country and part of the Himalayas, Doi Inthanon is known as "The Roof of Thailand". I went in January, a colder month, although freezing temperatures are an average all year around. I made it to the top! It is not an easy trek, but it makes for a good orientation to the higher altitude summits - and extreme ironists do not go for easy!

Within Doi Inthanon there are hill tribes. The most memorable extreme ironing moment I had was visiting with the Lahu and Karen Hill Tribes. One of the things I found so impressive, was how crisp their clothing looked, especially the woman elders. They were unimpressed by my iron and board as if they had been going about it a better way all these years.

Tabletop ironing boards are great for global locations. They can be easily fastened to a waist belt attached to your backpack that carries an iron.

Here is a list of extreme and global ironing locations:

Doi Inthanon, Thailand

Mount Fuji, Japan

Petra, Jordon

Mehlweg Mountain, Austria

Bolivia Salt Flats, Bolivia

Snowdonia National Park, Wales

Blue Lagoon, Iceland

Enchanted Forest, Scotland

Roman Baths, England

Cliffs of Moher, Ireland

Grand Canyon, Arizona

Red Rock Canyon, Nevada (beginner rock climbers)

Hueco Tanks State Historical Site, Texas (advanced rock climbers)

Red River Gorge, Kentucky (advanced rock climbers)

Shawangunk Mountains, New York (advanced rock climbers)

Scuba Diving

When I first started extreme ironing, I thought all the scuba diving ironists were part of a group of ironists gone rouge. But in the world of extreme ironing, where no rules are the only rules, it is all part of the family.

You will not be plugging in when scuba diving. When an ironist tells you they 'plugged in', that means they connected their iron to a power source. If you are in water or touching water, you do not want to plug in. You will electrocute yourself. Do not do it!

Most ironists will choose not to plug in at times. Scuba diving would be one of those times.

In the last section I mentioned Koh Bida Nok, my first experience extreme ironing underwater. Before I share my experience with you, let me tell you, every time I dive I feel like I am being transported into a Tim Burton film, entering a world of fluidity. I love scuba diving! Seems unsurpassable, right? You haven't tried extreme ironing while scuba diving! Twenty meters below the surface, surrounded by schools of yellow snapper and black tip reef sharks, balancing my tabletop board and iron, it is a deeper kind of enchantment -literally and metaphorically. You become so small, a grain of sand in the vastness that surrounds you. It is peace. Peacefulness at its elementary level. I have experienced more meditative moments extreme ironing underwater than I have doing yoga.

But, before I experienced those moments, I went through some trial and error. On this dive, I used a full-size ironing board. Big mistake! Do not try to use a full-size board the first couple times you attempt to extreme iron while underwater. The most you will get out of it is a selfie like this, while ascending early due to a loose board retrieval.

If you are new to extreme ironing, like I was here, use a tabletop ironing board and a full-size iron with a retractable cord. The best type of equipment to dive with. If you can find a travel size iron with a retractable cord, get it and use it! A retractable cord while diving is a must. Since you are not plugging in, do not let the cord dangle. You could damage coral, harm fish and other marine life.

Don't worry about simulating the 'real thing', everyone will know if you are under water, you are not really plugged in.

I also chose not to compensate for the 'extra weight' by not using less weights on my weight belt. This is a personal decision. I am very petite; typically, I add more weights on my second dive of the day. I also find the equipment to be very light, even when using a full-size board and iron. Because of this, I use my usual weight amount every time. Everybody will feel a little differently about this, but, make sure you can still maintain buoyancy with the addition of your board and iron. The most important thing to remember when extreme ironing underwater, is to make sure you have a free hand for equalizing. When I first started diving, taking my GoPro was out of the question, I had to focus on my equalizing and buoyancy.

Invest in a Lightweight Waterproof Dry Sack. They have a fastened clip that looks like this:

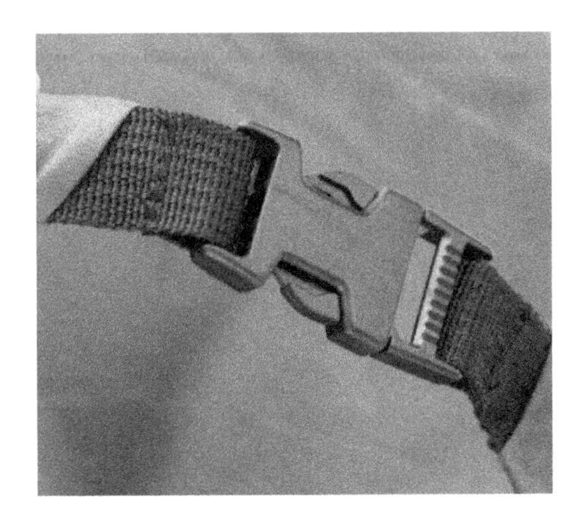

They are very easy to fasten and remove. Use this to store your iron until you reach your desired depth and are ready to start extreme ironing underwater. You can find a Lightweight Waterproof Dry Sack on eBay and Amazon for less than $20. It has waterproof as part of its name, but it does not need to be waterproof since you will be opening it up under water. If you choose to use something else, avoid strings and anything that can harm you and marine life.

My Thailand divemaster, never goes on a dive without a Lightweight Waterproof Dry Sack. In it, he puts an inflatable signaling device and an inflatable distress flag along with other emergency items. I recommend carrying one of your own. You can find both devices online or contact your local dive shop. If you are under water and get lost from your group or have an emergency, instead of coming up to the surface in open water, if you can, move in the direction of the reef before ascending. Then, inflate your emergency flag. Typically, more water traffic happens closer to the reefs. In these cases, coming up to the surface near a reef is a lot safer than ascending in open water.

Here are some extreme ironing diving locations:

Dryer Island and Geyser Rock, South Africa (an ultimate extreme ironist experience)

Barracuda Point, Malaysia

Yongala, Australia

Cod Hole, Australia

Great Blue Hole, Belize

Koh Bida Nok, Thailand

Malong, Thailand

Kailua Kona, Hawaii

Elphinstone Reef, Egyptian Red Sea

Raja Ampat Islands, Indonesia

Misool's Boo Rocks, Indonesia

Baranof Island, Alaska (jellyfish dive)

If you are curious about my South Africa selections at the top, give all the credit to the great white sharks. Yes! That is right! Dryer and Geyser Rock Island are home to the great whites. After you become a skilled extreme ironist, you are going to want to continue to challenge yourself. That is what extreme sports are all about. It is not all about the adrenaline, the sharp piercing tingles through your body and the analgesic result. It is not about becoming heighten then numb. It is about connecting with the forces that surround us, awakening our mind, our soul, living among the elements, transcending to awareness, challenging ourselves, and most importantly having fun!

Chapter 3: Extreme Ironing Equipment

As in most anything in life, being equipped properly is essential to success. One of my first experiences with extreme ironing was in the park. I had a 6x2 metal ironing board that had a loose lever. Its precarious disposition led to it to continually release the latch, causing the hallow metal legs to flap back and forth while I was walking through the park. The 25 yards I had to walk from my car to my extreme ironing spot, felt like a football field times one-hundred. There was no end to the flapping. I had one hand holding my 5lb iron and the other was trying to gain some traction with my board. In hindsight, I should have stop and readjusted everything. But, it felt like the whole city was staring at me. All I could think of doing, at the time, was to walk faster and repeat, "excuse me, sorry, excuse me, sorry" to anyone in proximity of my flapping board legs. Yes, not a good look. Equipment matters!

Ironing Board, Iron, Clothing (something to iron), Shoes, Extension Cord & Generator (both are optional).

This is a list of basic equipment you will need to get started. Jot the list down and let's go shopping!

Ironing Boards

Before selecting a board, if your goal is to enter competitions, check their requirements first. You will save on time and unnecessary expenses this way. Some competitions require you to use a board with a length minimum of 3.3 feet or a full-size board at 4.5 feet.

While it may be best to use novice equipment in training, depending on the requirements, you might be able to find equipment that meets a novice needs and the competition requirements.

Your board needs to be stable, operational, durable, light, compact, and have a thick padded board cover. This should be your go-to criteria for the ironing board you choose. Each one is going to be essential to successful extreme ironing.

The first thing to do is go to your local big-box store. A couple places to try are Target or if you are in the UK, try Argos, and for my Canada friends try The Bay. These are just suggestions; the goal is to find a store near you that carries a decent amount of ironing boards. You want to hold one in your hands. This will be your baseline and help you gauge what is right for you. Open it up in the store and look at the feet, most stable footing will have straight footing on one side of the board and curvature footing on the other.

This will become important when placing your board down at an angle, on rough terrain, and when dealing with various weather conditions.

These are my favorite boards to use because I want a majority of the focus to be on my balance, not the balance of the board. I have found, that the slight curvature footing at one side of the board helps towards balancing the ironing board better, making it more versatile for a variety of extreme ironing locations.

Here is another picture of one of my first extreme ironing experiences. The ironing board I am using has straight legs on both sides. And yes, you guessed it, my board was sliding every few seconds. It would have made my extreme ironing a lot easier if I would have known to get an ironing board with curvature footing on one side. Another great thing about the boards with curvature footing on one side, they tend to weigh a lot less than the boards that have straight legs on both sides.

You can also go with ironing boards that have double legs on each side.

This is another one I like to use and is equally as stable as my first choice. These boards tend to weigh a lot more, but most of them come with a great side tray accessory. The side tray is removal and comes in handy when extreme ironing in places like the subway or town square; you can set your iron down in between your ironing sets. If you are planning on doing extreme ironing in urban locations, this one will work.

As for the ironing boards with a straight bar footing on both sides, while not my favorite, do not completely discount them. These can be great for skiing and snowboarding. The straight bar feet can easily be fastened to the ski's or placed in boots and glide down a slope with you. In these extreme ironing locations, you want to glide. Having the straight footing on both sides of your board will not work against you.

Another type of ironing board is the tabletop ironing board. You do not have to worry about flapping legs with these. Tabletop ironing boards are ideal for extreme ironing while cycling, on a motorbike, skydiving, whitewater rafting, or something comparable. And as I mentioned in the last chapter, this is also a great board for any newcomer that wants to combine extreme ironing with scuba diving. One of the reasons I really like this board for scuba diving is that it is minimal. I like to be mindful of marine life and try to introducc thc lcast possiblc. Remember, be sure that anything you take down, you can bring back up.

Now that you have decided on what kind of board you want and evaluated stability, check the operational mechanics. You do not want to have an operational malfunction during your extreme ironing venture. Check for an easy to use lever and a secure latch. Some ironing boards have locks on both side of the legs, but be careful when settling on one of these. You do not want too complicated. Think about what locations you will be at while doing extreme ironing and make sure you feel comfortable with the mechanics of your board.

Lastly, go for light, compact, and a thick padded cover. The thick padded cover allows you to establish a better much press on your clothing. If your board does not have a thick one, you can always order one online.

Try Amazon, Bed Bath & Beyond, or Wayfair.com for thick ironing board covers. These can range anywhere from $10.00 to $30.00.

The most important thing is that you are comfortable with your board. Hold a couple boards at your side, try opening them up and holding it at different angles before buying.

Note: for a reference on the ironing boards with curvature footing on one side you can look up, Homz Contour Steel Top Ironing Board - Extra Stable Legs on Amazon.com or Real Simple Ironing Board on Bedbathandbeyond.com.

Irons

Your iron should have a steam feature, non-stick soleplate with steam holes, lightweight, and be stainless steel or titanium (lighter weighing option). In most cases you want your iron to have 1500-2,000 wattage, unless opting for a small travel iron, in which case you will have to sacrifice the wattage.

Wattage is important because you want to be able to iron well and be timely about it. The higher the wattage the better chance of a better press.

Notice I did not mention a clean feature in the above iron criteria. This is because, you do not need a clean feature on your iron. I usually avoid irons with this feature. The clean feature has a lot of room for error and can end up ruining your clothing. In chapter 4 I will go over some easy alternatives to keeping your iron soleplate clean.

My favorite irons to use are irons with retractable cords or travel irons. Retractable cords are good for every extreme ironing location. I consider them to be the universal go-to iron for all extreme ironing experiences. My other favorite iron to use is the travel iron. This one works great for all my random extreme ironing ventures. When I am not scuba diving or rock climbing, I will use my travel iron. And, like I mentioned in the last chapter, if you can find a travel iron with a retractable cord, get it!

Some people use cordless irons. These come with a heating element that require an electric receptacle. Once taken off the heating element you will have a limited time with the iron before it cools. I do not recommend these irons for beginners or solo extreme ironists.

Unfortunately, battery operated irons still have a long way to go. If you can find one that works good, I'd get it. These can be found on China Amazon or you can get on board with extreme and take a 17-hour flight from the United States and track one down.

Most of your iron selection is about personal preference - how well it holds in your hand and what is best for your extreme ironing locations.

Clothing

The first pieces of clothing I chose to use were my cotton t-shirts. I wanted to start simple, because, I honestly did not know what I was getting myself into. I typically use cotton or cotton mixed material. Once you are ready to take it to the next level, mix it up -try silk or wool! Extreme ironing is about taking what you would normally do and adding the extreme. So, if you have a certain piece of clothing that needs to be ironed, forget about playing it safe and go for it! Just be sure to know what you are working with, be familiar with your ironing settings and the material. Then, iron it out!

Footwear

If you are thinking footwear is a tad random to cover, read on! I am sure you will thank me later.

Most extreme sports have footwear requirements. In fact, depending on your industry of employment, most employers have footwear requirements as well. Appropriate footwear is universal. You will not make it far in rock climbing, if you are wearing a pair of converse.

A couple years ago I went back to my hometown of Okinawa and made my way to the beach. I was ready to take extreme ironing on in the ocean of Okinawa. I ran into the water and after getting about thigh high, I started to scream. Thinking back on this moment, I should have walked or at least jogged. But since I ran, the sensation of sharp shells and coral penetrating the bottom of my feet, didn't hit me until it was too late. The pain must have somehow jolted my memory because, at that moment, I started to have flashbacks to my childhood when my family and I would go out on a fishing boat and at 4-5 feet deep, the bottom of the ocean would be covered in eels. How did I forget?!?!

Don't let the internet pictures or reviews fool you. Okinawa shore lines and ocean floors are covered in shells, rocks, and coral. Regardless of what water activity you will be doing, finding a good pair of water shoes is important. I use these shoes all the time:

I found these Body Glove water shoes on Amazon. They cost less than $20.00 and are extremely comfortable. The outsole of the shoe is thick with grips for traction and they are incredibly light. I will even use them when I am scuba diving, by replacing my diving boots with them. I am more comfortable in them; and if I ever want to remove my fins and walk around, I can. I recommend getting these or something comparable to these for water activities.

For those of you that want to do extreme ironing while trekking or rock climbing, Solomons, Boreal, and Madrock are great brands that I use. Most brands will have footwear that will complement a variety of budgets. You want something that will withstand all the elements. A good pair of shoes will have a base price of about $130 and go up from there. Don't shy away from the investment, especially if you are going to be doing any mountainous extreme ironing.

While you are trying on footwear, ask the store representative about protective eyewear, handwear and headwear. Know your location and be equipped!

Extension Cord & Generator

Some extreme ironists chose not to plug in. This makes the extension cord and generator optional for ironists. Before purchasing these two items, try extreme ironing a couple times. Ask yourself 'what type of locations do you want to cross off your list?' or 'what sport will you combine with extreme ironing?' and 'what type of extreme ironist do you want to be?'.

Many sceptics of extreme ironing are critical of ironists that do not plug in, but that should not discourage you from choosing one way or another. Frankly, these critics are not fond of extreme ironing all together. I chose to do both depending on my location, and I am not alone, most ironist will do both.

If you decide to plug in, Amazon has a great selection of outdoor extension cords. Coleman Cable Vinyl Outdoor Extension Cord is 50 feet for $15.54 on amazon. The same brand has one that is 100 feet for $27.60. You'll want to make sure you purchase an outdoor extension cord; outdoor extension cords are made to withstand all the elements unlike the indoor ones.

As for a generator, surprisingly, there are a lot of small portable ones that are reasonably priced. Home Depot has a great selection. You can find Power Pro Technology Portable Generator at HomeDepot.com. It has 900-1000 wattage and weighs less than 36 pounds. You can purchase it for $139.53 with free shipping options. Shop around for generators. This is a great investment. A compact generator will come in handy for all kinds of situations. I invested in one a couple months after I started extreme ironing and it has been one of my best investments. I have used mine to charge my phone and blow dry my hair during power outages. It is a multi-purpose item! Don't forget to consider the wattage of both your iron and generator. Make sure the wattage is high enough to handle your iron and if sharing, the irons of others. If you have a 2000 wattage iron you will need to find a portable generator that is above that wattage amount. When comparing wattage, it is best to have your generator be generously above the amount of wattage you think you will need.

Chapter 4: Extreme Ironing Tips

Let's talk ironing. Eventually, most ironists will find a way of ironing that is best for them. Until then, I'll share a few tips that will help you along the way.

The first tip is to keep your iron clean. Earlier I mentioned, I like to forgo the clean feature on my iron. Instead, I use a metal ball scrubber and water. This has always done well for me. You can get a pack of metal ball scrubbers for less than $2.00 at your local store. If your iron is severally scorched, try replacing the water with vinegar. Dampen your scrubber and use circular motion to clean the plate.

Second, fill a water bottle with water and bring it with you. This will not be for your hydration, although, do not forgot to hydrate. This water will be for your iron. You do not want to fill your iron with water and pack it in your bag. Most likely, the water will end up all over the bottom of your bag. Once you are on location with your extreme ironing equipment and ready to get started, pour the water into your iron water reservoir. You want to be able to use the steam feature. Depending on how small your compartment is and how much ironing you will be doing, keep an extra reserve and fill up as needed.

Third, keep the iron water reservoir clean. Every two weeks, pour a mixture of half water and half vinegar into the water compartment. Plug the iron in and heat it up as you normally would. After several minutes of steaming, unplug and let the water drain out naturally. You will want to position the iron face down while draining. The best thing to do is find a heat resistant tray and be sure to standby. Once fully drained, fill the reservoir up with water and repeat all the previous steps. Before using the iron on clothing, do a test run on a small part of a towel, this will confirm the iron does not have any remaining vinegar that will stain your clothes.

Fourth, if you are ironing dress shirts starch spray goes a long way. You can pick some up at a local store.

Fifth, turn your piece of clothing inside out. This will aid in a crisp finished look.

Sixth, start your ironing in this sequence: collar, cuffs, sleeves, body of shirt. If you are ironing pants, shorts, skirts, or dresses, start at the top and work your way down to the legs or bottom of clothing.

Lastly, if you are short on ideas for what sport to mix with extreme ironing, here is a list of some extreme sports ironists have combined with extreme ironing:

Mountain biking

Motorcycling

Cycling

Unicycling

Ziplining

Skydiving

Microlighting

Hang gliding

Parasailing

White water rafting

Water skiing

Surfing

Canoeing

Kayaking

Stand-up paddle boarding

Wakeboarding

Windsurfing

Coasteering

Ice skating

Roller blading

Free diving

Scuba diving

Skiing

Snowboarding

Horseback riding

Tree climbing

Rock climbing

Mountain climbing

Spelunking

Reference the above list for ideas. If you are going to decide on one of the above or something similar, be sure to experience it on its own at least couple times before combining it with extreme ironing. If you are a first timer to an extreme sport, practice extreme ironing and another sport separately. Once you fill comfortable enough, you can combine the two.

Extreme Ironing Accessories

After you try extreme ironing a few times, you'll want to start considering accessories. These are the two major accessories that I carry with me:

Tie Down also known as Universal Tie Down and Selfie Stick or Camera Tripod.

A Tie Down is like a flat rope.

You can find Sport Rack 18-Feet Universal Tie Down on Amazon, and something comparable at REI, Backcountry, or stores similar to these. The average price for one of these is $20.00. Ironists use the Tie

Down to wrap around the ironing board. You will need one pair or one long one. The idea is to use the Tie Down over each side of your ironing board legs. This will secure the legs of your board and insure it stays it its folded position.

The other useful accessory is a selfie stick or camera tripod. The one I use is called Flexible Tripod Selfie Stick. These are great because you can wrap them around a tree, bridge railing, or your wrist. The Flexible Tripod Selfie Stick can be found on eBay for $21.00. This works great for extreme ironing beginners. The flexible tripod legs allow you to attach it to most anything that is around you.

Extreme Ironing Starter Kit

Eventually, there will come a time where you will need all the things I mentioned in this book. But, if you are a real beginner, I want to simplify it even more. I have put together a startup kit for you. For your first several extreme ironing experiences, you will be able to get by with this extreme ironing starter kit. Once you have graduated from the novice extreme ironing level, keep the starter kit handy for random extreme ironing ventures!

Tabletop ironing board, travel iron, flexible tripod selfie stick.

Honey-Can-Do Tabletop Ironing Board with Retractable Iron Rest from Amazon. It is $20.90.

Steamfast (SF717) Home-and-Away Mini Steam Iron from Amazon. It is $23.63.

Flexible Tripod Selfie Stick from eBay. It is $21.00. Occasionally, you can find the same one on Groupon.com and LivingSocial.com for $7.00 to $10.00.

You are now ready to take on extreme ironing!

Extreme Ironing Training

Now that you are ready to become an extreme ironist, know that training will be continuous. Some extreme ironists have extreme ironed in trees, others have extreme ironed between giant gorges and below ice. It takes training. "Every skill you acquire doubles your odds of success" – Scott Adams.

Every extreme ironing experience will help build your skills and make you a better extreme ironist. When training, look for things you can improve. Did you shy away from a public place? Next time, challenge yourself by heading to the town square. Did you climb a tree half way? Try climbing higher.

Planning is another important aspect of training. Think ahead – 'what is your location?', 'did you pack all the accessories listed in this book?', 'do you have all the protective gear you need?'.

This book should help you skip all the trial and error moments extreme ironists have, but, that isn't a guarantee you will not have your days. Even the most experienced ironists have their unsuccessful stories. The important thing is to keep going. Keep training! Eventually, you will reach the master level of extreme ironing!

Chapter 5: Extreme Ironing Competitions, Tournaments, & Networking

Competitions & Tournaments

Competitions have aided in legitimizing extreme ironing as a real extreme sport. I took Brazilian Jiu-Jitsu classes for two months; for me, extreme ironing competitions are like earning the solid red belt. Every legitimate extreme sport needs competitions and tournaments. Extreme ironists may have some time before this extreme sport heads to the Olympics, but that has not stopped ironists from establishing medals and trophies of their own.

Local pockets of ironists hold competitions all around the world. The first Extreme Ironing World Championship was in Germany, 2002. In this multinational competition, over 70 ironists competed. In 2003 the Rowenta Trophy Tournament challenged extreme ironists across the globe to submit pictures of their most extreme ironing experiences. Over 150 ironists participated in the tournament. So far, the prices have included medals, trophies, laundry soup, a washing machine, small cash prizes, and a short vacation. Extreme ironists hope this list will grow as extreme ironing gains new members every year.

In 2011, extreme ironing claimed renown fame in the Guinness World Records. The record states there where 173 extreme ironists under water in the Netherlands; making it the most extreme ironists underwater at the same time.

While there has only been one Extreme Ironing World Championship, the future of this extreme sport is bright. All around the world ironists have created numerous local groups, compctitions, tournaments, tours, and unofficial records. In the next section, I will cover how to network with some of these groups, but you can also start your own!

Networking

Hashtag Extreme Ironing! That's right, hashtag extreme ironing is on Instagram at 1,579 hashtags and climbing. Scroll through the tags. You will find fellow ironists and newcomers looking to take on extreme ironing, some, even asking if anyone is interested in teaming up with them. Check it out and start connecting!

In chapter one I mentioned Maki Sugimoto and a TEDx Talks video he did on extreme ironing. The YouTube video is called "Extreme Ironing Motivates and Inspires Your People by TEDx Kagoshima University". It is a 17-minute video about Maki's experience with extreme ironing.

You can watch the video by using the link below:

https://www.youtube.com/watch?v=0jJLyvNn_to&vl=ja

Maki founded Extreme Ironist Club. You can find the clubs social media page on Facebook. Maki can also be found on Facebook and Instagram by using his full name, Maki Sugimoto.

De Montfort University Leicester (DMU), has an Instagram page under DMUIron and you can find Phil Shaw on Facebook at Extreme Ironing Official.

Here is a list of additional Extreme Ironists Groups and Resources:

Extreme Ironing Bureau (info@extremeironing.com)

German Extreme Ironing Section

English Extreme Ironing Bureau

Ironing.de

Extremeironing.me

Don't be shy, extreme ironists love to connect with other extreme ironists. Browse the hashtags, reach out to fellow ironists, and create your own extreme ironists local chapter!

Chapter 6: Extreme Ironing First Aid

Extreme Ironing First Aid

I use REI mountain series hiker medical kit or their tactical field trauma kit. You can also make your own, but these kits come with instructions, letting you know when and how to use what is inside of them. Check your kit and make sure you have a tourniquet, if not, you can find one on Amazon or AEDSuperstore.com. I also purchase normal saline. You can purchase this at your local pharmacy or online on a reputable site. Normal saline is sodium chloride (salt) and water. It is one of the first things a medical professional will connect you to when you are admitted to a hospital or injured. It is also used to clean an open skin injury.

Since you will be working with heat, have some instant cold packs handy. These are like ice packs that do not need to be kept in a freezer. When you need them, you shake and squeeze the pack. Instantly, the pack will become cold and you can place it on the closed injured site. You can purchase them at your local store.

Always have some first aid items handy. You never think you will need it, until you do.

As in any other extreme sport, have a friend with you and let people know what your plans are. In the scuba diving world, we use the buddy system but this is something that should be universal when it comes to all extreme sports.

Chapter 7: Extreme Ironing Olympics

Extreme Ironing Olympics

In previous decades adding new sports to the Olympics were full of formalities. But, not anymore. Times have changed. Thanks to development of social media and other media platforms, many organizations like the Olympics are feeling the pressure of their audience. Decades ago, no one predicted BMX and skateboarding would one day meet the Olympic lineup with archery and swimming. Audience demand has opened new doors for extreme sports and the International Olympic Committee is listening.

Extreme ironing has a global following, with thousands of ironists all around. According to the Olympic requirements, extreme ironing still needs an International Sports Federation. Until then, there is a lot that can be done to increase awareness and influence in favor of extreme ironing.

In order for extreme ironing to gain recognition, ironists need to continue to extreme iron, use their social media #extremeiron #extremeironing and involve their local media. If you cannot find a competition or tournament near you, create one!

The Olympics for extreme ironing may not be far off!

About the Expert

Marie Claire Medina has spent over five years working as a freelance writer and editor. Born in Hiroshima, Japan, she spent her early childhood years living in between Japan and Okinawa. It was at this early stage in life, where Marie Claire discovered her passion for global cultures and writing. Since then, she has focused on traveling and using her travels to provide her writing with more authenticity and versatility. She is devoted to learning, experiencing, and having a sense of humor.

HowExpert publishes quick 'how to' guides on all topics from A to Z by everyday experts. Visit HowExpert.com to learn more.

Recommended Resources

- HowExpert.com – Quick 'How To' Guides on All Topics from A to Z by Everyday Experts.
- HowExpert.com/free – Free HowExpert Email Newsletter.
- HowExpert.com/books – HowExpert Books
- HowExpert.com/courses – HowExpert Courses
- HowExpert.com/membership – HowExpert Membership Site
- HowExpert.com/writers – Write About Your #1 Passion/Knowledge/Expertise & Become a HowExpert Author.
- HowExpert.com/resources – Additional HowExpert Recommended Resources
- YouTube.com/HowExpert – Subscribe to HowExpert YouTube.
- Instagram.com/HowExpert – Follow HowExpert on Instagram.
- Facebook.com/HowExpert – Follow HowExpert on Facebook.

CPSIA information can be obtained
at www.ICGtesting.com
Printed in the USA
BVHW041121301219
568134BV00009B/53/P